Parish
Acolyte
Guide

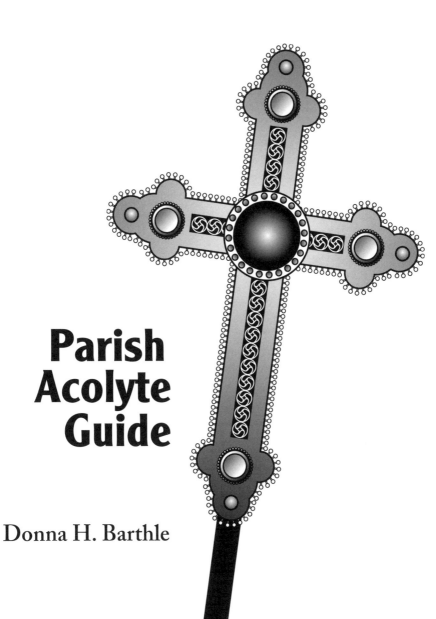

Parish
Acolyte
Guide

Donna H. Barthle

MOREHOUSE PUBLISHING
A Continuum imprint
HARRISBURG • LONDON • NEW YORK

Morehouse Publishing
P.O. Box 13321
Harrisburg, PA 17105

Morehouse Publishing is a Continuum imprint.

Graphic Design by Wesley Hoke

Library of Congress Cataloging-in-Publication Data

Barthle, Donna H.
  The parish acolyte guide / by Donna H. Barthle.
     p. cm.
Includes bibliographical references.
  ISBN 0-8192-1938-X (pbk.)
  1. Acolytes--Episcopal Church--Handbooks, manuals, etc. 2. Episcopal
Church--Liturgy--Handbooks, manuals, etc. I. Title.
  BX5948.B37 2003
  264'.03--dc21
                                        2003001332

Printed in the United States of America

05 06 07 08 6 5 4 3 2

Table of Contents

Dedication

This book is dedicated to the thousands of acolytes, of all ages, serving at altars in every country of the world. I am awed by your generosity of spirit and courage in serving others.

Acknowledgments

My thanks to the many acolytes and acolyte leaders, both ordained and lay, who freely shared their knowledge and parish traditions to help prepare this book.

I am particularly grateful to the "pros" who unstintingly shared their time, knowledge, and advice, including Pastor Belvin Brummett, rector of St. Peter's Lutheran Church, Bowie, Texas, and the Reverend Andrew Sherman, rector of the Episcopal Memorial Church of the Prince of Peace, Gettysburg, Pennsylvania.

My special thanks to the Reverend Bonnie Vandelinder, librarian of the Gettysburg Lutheran Seminary and associate priest for the Prince of Peace Church, for both her wit and penchant for accuracy.

Introduction

Welcome to the ministry of acolytes. You are an important part of the life and ministry of the church.

Acolytes are part of an old and honored ministry as servants to God and his Church. The word "acolyte" does, after all, mean "one who serves." The most important qualifications for joining the ministry are enthusiasm and a willingness to serve and to learn.

Acolytes around the world share a common history (Chapter 1), common vestments and equipment (Chapter 2), and even basic duties (Chapter 3). The way those duties are performed, however, may vary from church to church. Because parish acolyte programs are different depending on parish traditions, the preferences of the particular priest you serve, and even the physical design of church buildings, space has been left in Chapters 4 through 7 for you to add details and cues specific to your parish.

This book is dedicated to your needs and designed to help you fully understand not only what we do, but how we do it and, just as importantly, why. If you have questions while you review this book, please ask your acolyte leader or parish priest.

In Peace,

Donna H. Barthle
Gettysburg, Pennsylvania
January 2, 2003

Chapter 1
A Short History of the Acolyte Ministry

The ministry of acolytes exists at the heart of our worship services. The ministry itself, the vestments, the titles, and the duties acolytes perform in assisting a priest to prepare for the mystery that is the Holy Eucharist are directly tied to almost two thousand years of history. Borrowing from an old expression, you can't know where you're going if you don't know where you've been.

The term acolyte comes from the Greek word *akolouthos*, meaning "follower" or "attendant." Although some people believe that the history of acolytes traces back to Samuel in the Old Testament, the first written historical record of the term appears in a letter from Pope Cornelius to the Bishop of Antioch in the year 251 CE. In this letter, the pope lists the clergy of Rome, which included forty-two acolytes.

In the early history of the church, acolytes were one of four lower orders of the clergy. The primary purpose of the order was to prepare young men for the priesthood. Their duties included lighting and extinguishing candles, carrying candles in procession, taking charge of the alms basin, helping the priest prepare for the Eucharist, and generally fetching and carrying. References in early texts also reveal that some acolytes carried consecrated (or blessed) bread to other churches, took Communion to the sick and imprisoned, and helped prepare and examine candidates for Baptism or Confirmation.

Between the fifth and ninth centuries, in a series of ancient directions to the clergy known as the *Ordines Romani*, acolyte duties are described and include the information that acolytes led and organized processions preceding the pope. In the same time period, we also see the predecessor of modern gospel processions as two acolytes carried candles to accompany the reader and ensure that he had enough light to see the text.

A favorite story concerns the acolyte Tarsicus. In the year 258 CE, the Roman Emperor Valerian decreed that bishops and priests were to sacrifice to the Roman gods and were forbidden to hold services. The penalty for violation of this decree was death. While taking the consecrated bread from the Pope to churches in the city of Rome, Tarsicus was stopped by a group of soldiers who wanted to see what he was concealing. He refused to show them the sacred bread and was beaten to death on the spot.

The involvement of young people and teenagers in the ministry isn't apparent until the ninth century at the Synod of Mainz, where it was declared that every priest should have a cleric or a boy to read the lessons and assist him in the services. This changed three things in church history. First, young people were allowed to serve the altar. Second, the training of these assistants was left to the individual priest. And third, there was no requirement for these lay assistants to train for or eventually join the priesthood. This is apparently where the parallel ministry of altar boys emerged, although acolytes as an order of the church did not disappear.

After Martin Luther posted his Ninety-five Theses on the door of the Palast Church in Wittenberg, Germany, in 1517, few references to acolytes are found, and the ministry may have declined, possibly as a reaction against all things "Roman." The history of acolytes is further confused by the breakaway of other denominations, especially the formation of the Anglican Church when Henry VIII of England split the English Church from the Church of Rome in 1531.

During the Oxford movement in the early 1830s, the Anglican Church began a slow return to more traditional practices, and the ministry of acolytes began to reappear. The ministry all but disappeared for a time in the Lutheran Church but has recently been revived and is steadily growing in popularity as lay involvement in the church increases. In the Roman Catholic Church, while altar boys and girls are firmly established in their slightly limited roles, the ministry of acolytes still exists today as a separate ministry.

Girls and women were admitted to this all-male ministry in the late 1970s and early 1980s. Their admittance probably was influenced by the women's liberation movement and the ordination of women into the priesthood of the Episcopal Church in 1979 and in the Lutheran Church a few years earlier in the same decade. Another strong influence may have been shrinking family size and the resulting shortage of boys in the right age group. Whether of necessity or because of cultural rebellion, women and girls entered the ministry and were fully integrated by the 1990s in most Episcopal parishes. Most, although not all, Roman Catholic parishes now also assign girls to work on the altar.

Acolytes today remain servants of the altar. No matter the parish or even denominational differences, the primary duty of an acolyte remains to serve God and the Church, and to assist the priest in whatever way he or she needs or prefers. Electricity, instead of candles, now lights a very different altar than Christians of the year 251 C.E. were accustomed to seeing. Those same Christians might easily recognize, however, the humble figure at the foot of the altar dressed in cassock or alb and doing many of the same jobs as his or her predecessor of nearly two thousand years ago.

Chapter 2
Identifying Equipment and Vestments

Every vestment and piece of equipment on the altar has a specific purpose and a significance that in some cases goes back centuries, but in other cases may be the result of practical invention in your specific parish. This discussion will touch on and briefly describe a broad range, although not all, of the vestments and equipment commonly used in parish churches. Every parish is a little different, and a comprehensive review would require an entire book.

Vestments for Acolytes, Priests, and Deacons

Acolytes wear one of two types of vestment, either the cassock and cotta or surplice, or the server's alb. Both serve to cover street clothes and help keep the attention of both the acolyte and the congregation on worship rather than on the latest fashion.

Cassock: A simple robe with a high split collar, fitted at the shoulders and sleeves and falling straight to the ankle with no elaborate tucks or gathers. It is usually worn with a surplice or cotta. The traditional color for acolyte cassocks is red, the color of celebration. The priest's cassock is most often black. The cassock was originally the outer garment worn by a priest.

Surplice or cotta: A loose-fitting overgarment with bell sleeves. It is usually white and made of gathered material attached to a rounded or square yoke. A surplice or cotta is worn over the cassock. Acolytes and choir generally wear the shorter cotta. An acolyte's sleeves are often shortened to keep them from catching on vessels or equipment as the acolyte works. Priests most often wear the longer cathedral-length surplice with full-length sleeves. The historical purpose of a surplice or cotta was to keep

Cassock, cotta, and alb with cincture

the cassock clean during the working part of the service, which is why, in many parishes, the acolyte still performs any duties before the entry procession and after the exit procession without wearing the cotta.

Server's alb: A simple, long, loose-fitting robe with sleeves, with or without a hood. It is tied at the waist with a rope belt called a cincture. The alb is generally white or flax colored, although some parishes now use other colors. In monastic history, the alb was the simple clothing of religious orders. Priests may also wear an alb as a basic garment to cover street clothing under clerical vestments. Historically, the acolyte's vestments concealed or covered differences in social status, ensured that only relatively clean outer clothing was worn to approach the altar, and kept the wearer warm in unheated stone churches.

Cincture: This is the long rope belt tied around the waist of an alb. Acolytes usually tie this in a simple square or slipknot on the right side with the ends hanging fairly even. Priests also wear the cincture but tie it differently.

Pectoral cross or pendant: Many acolytes wear a cross of wood or metal or a pendant particular to their parish while serving the altar as a reminder to themselves and others of their duties. The server's cross is usually three to four inches in length and worn on a cord long enough so the cross hangs over the wearer's heart.

Chasuble: A chasuble is a priest's vestment worn for eucharistic services. Similar to a poncho, it hangs from the shoulders, has no specific sleeves, and may be oval or rectangular. Depending on style, it may have a collar or cowl. If there is more than one priest at a service, the primary celebrant wears the chasuble. Historical accounts disagree as to the origin and symbolism behind both the chasuble and the stole but most include the fact that the chasuble designated the primary celebrant at the Eucharist and provided extra warmth. The usual colors match the church seasons, for example, green, white, blue, and red.

Stole: This is a priest's vestment worn for sacramental services. The stole is a long, narrow cloth worn draped around the neck and hanging loose from both shoulders to about the knees. It may or may not be color-coded to match the colors of the altar hangings and the church seasons. Deacons also wear a stole when assisting with sacramental services, but deacons wear it across the chest and crossed or loosely knotted at the hip like a sash. As an alternative, deacons wearing a Byzantine stole wear it across the chest but cross or knot it at the shoulder with the longer, loose ends hanging at the front and back.

Cope: Also a priest's vestment, but unlike the chasuble, a cope looks more like a cape and closes in the front across the chest. Copes are often worn by bishops but may also be worn by priests, deacons, or the laity on special or festive occasions. They are generally quite elaborate.

Dalmatic: A dalmatic is a deacon's vestment generally worn over an alb for services. The color generally varies with the church seasons, as do the chasuble and altar hangings. However, the deacon's vestment is more tailored than a chasuble and has sleeves.

On the Altar, You Will Find ...

Chalice and paten: The chalice is the cup used to hold the wine and water. The paten is the small plate used to hold the host bread during the Eucharist. You may hear the terms communion cup or common cup for the chalice, and bread plate or tray instead of paten. The chalice and paten are usually a matched set and may be stored together under a veil on the altar (see veil later in this section) before and during services. In some parishes, the chalice and paten are kept on the credence table until they are needed in the service and are returned there afterward.

**Chalice, paten, service book, and
gospel book on the altar**

Gospel book: The book of gospel readings used during the service.

Candles: Candles, in general, represent the light of Christ in the world. The two larger candles on either edge of the altar are the eucharistic candles. On the left is the gospel candle (the gospel was traditionally read on that side of the church), and on the right is the epistle candle (the epistles or lessons were traditionally read on that side of the church). The Paschal candle, a large, decorated candle, generally in a separate stand, is used for the fifty days of Easter and for Baptisms, funerals, and other special occasions. The Paschal candle specifically represents the light of the risen Christ and is lighted for the first time each year during the Easter Vigil. Some parishes also use six additional candles, called service candles or office lights. These are lighted routinely for Morning Prayer and all other altar-based services. Office lights are most often used in churches where the altar is against the sanctuary wall or where a candle rail or shelf has been installed on the wall behind and above the altar. Other candles used in the service include Advent candles (usually in a wreath) and sanctuary lights (see page 13).

Service book: This is the prayer book used by the priest, which contains the service and rubrics (instructions for the priest) in print large enough to be read while conducting the service.

Cross or crucifix: On or above the altar, you will generally find a plain cross or crucifix (with a representation of the body of Christ) as a reminder that our faith is based on the life and resurrection of Christ.

Basic altar hangings: These usually include an altar cover in white linen or in the colors of the church seasons. If the cloth is in a color or fabric other than plain white linen, it may be called a "frontal." Lectern and pulpit hangings usually match the colors and symbols on the frontal.

Altar linens: The different linens can be confusing and for the most part the priest and altar guild will deal with them. But occasionally a replacement or extra piece of linen may be needed, and acolytes should be able to identify the basics without a great deal of fuss.

The "fair linen" is the long white, rectangular linen cloth on top of the altar cover.

A "purificator" is a small 12 by 12-inch linen napkin used to wipe the chalice after Communion, it is folded in thirds and may have a small cross embroidered on its face.

The "corporal" is a larger napkin (about 20 by 20 inches) that the priest places on the fair linen under the chalice and paten while he or she prepares the Eucharist. It generally has a cross embroidered in the center or in one corner and is also folded in thirds.

The "pall" is a small (7 by 7 inches) stiff white linen-covered square placed over the chalice when it is not in use.

The "veil" covers the chalice, paten, and pall before and after Communion while those vessels are on the altar. The veil may be white linen but is usually in colors that match the frontal and other hangings. A veil is not used if the chalice and paten are kept on the credence table.

The "burse" is a 9 by 9-inch folder or pocket that holds the service linens. It may also match the altar hangings or be made of white linen.

On the Credence Table, You Will Find ...

The "credence table cover" is smaller than the fair linen and often has a 2-inch embroidered cross.

The "host box," also called a breadbox, is generally a small silver, gold, or ceramic box with a lid, and contains the wafers to be consecrated during the Eucharist. In place of a host box, a ciborium, which is shaped like a chalice with a lid, may be used.

The two cruets, which can be made of glass, crystal, or ceramic, contain wine in one and water in the other. For large services, a large silver or ceramic flagon may be used to hold the wine.

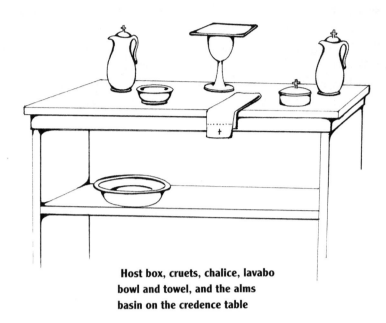

**Host box, cruets, chalice, lavabo
bowl and towel, and the alms
basin on the credence table**

The lavabo bowl and a lavabo towel (rectangular, about 10 by 15 inches) are used for the ceremonial washing of the priest's hands before the Eucharist. A second chalice covered by a purificator and pall may also be on the table if more than one chalice is needed for the service.

On the lower shelf or on a nearby table, you will usually find an alms basin and collection plates or baskets. The term "alms basin" actually applies to the large basin used to carry two or more stacked collection plates, however, the term may also be used to refer to the smaller basins or collection plates.

Other Equipment Acolytes Use

Torch or taper: Both terms refer to candles, generally wax or oil filled, that are carried in processions alone or are used to light the processional cross or the path of a visiting dignitary. If the candle is mounted on a staff, it is usually referred to as a torch. If in a candleholder, it is usually referred to as a taper. The term taper may also refer to the thin wax-covered wick in the candle lighter. Both terms are also used to refer to the acolyte who carries the candle.

Processional cross: This is a cross or crucifix mounted on a staff for processions. The processional cross, carried by a crucifer, generally leads the procession as a reminder that we are called to follow the cross. The entrance of the cross begins the formal worship service.

Sanctus bells: A group of four small bells attached to a single handle. Some parishes use a gong and mallet for the same purpose. The bells are used in many parishes to signal the celebration and presence of Christ in our midst during the Eucharist at the acclamation and at the elevation of the bread and wine. Long ago, when the services were conducted in Latin rather than in the language of the local population, the bells signaled the congregation at important moments in the service.

Sacristy bells: Sacristy bells are either a single bell or a set of three bells, usually attached to a cord and hung on the wall next to the door of the sacristy. The bells, usually rung by an acolyte, signal the entry of the clergy and the beginning of the service.

Thurible and boat: The thurible is a brass container designed to hold charcoal and incense. It usually has a chain

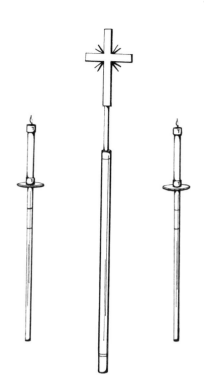

Torches and processional cross

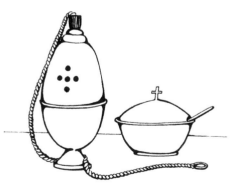

Thurible and boat with spoon

attached to either the sides or a lid so that it may be safely carried in procession. The boat, a small container with a spoon and lid, is used to carry extra incense to be used during the service. Incense has been used since biblical times as both an offering to God and to visually represent our prayers rising to God. A third biblical use was to cleanse or purify offerings to God. The traditional offerings include the alms, bread and wine, and even ourselves. (See eucharistic prayers, page 336, BCP.) Some churches today use incense routinely for eucharistic services. Some churches use it only for special occasions and others use incense rarely if at all.

Banners and flags: A banner is a cloth flag mounted horizontally instead of vertically so that its full face is always displayed. Banners display messages or symbols special to an occasion or to a

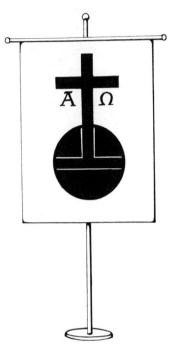

Banner and stand

particular group. The concept of banners goes back to the feudal period when each king or feudal lord had his family symbol or crest embroidered on banners hung from his castle walls and on smaller banners or flags carried with him as he traveled. Anyone approaching from a distance then knew whose forces controlled the castle, and those inside the castle could identify an approaching group before they were close enough to be a danger. Banners and flags (the cloth is vertical on the staff) are still used to identify many types of organizations. The Episcopal Church has its own specific flag (vertical like the U.S. flag), and many parishes have specific identifying banners.

Inside the Sanctuary Rail

The aumbry or tabernacle: Either term may be used to refer to the cabinet or case used to store the reserved consecrated elements. Priests or lay ministers use the reserved elements when taking Communion to those who are sick or unable to attend the service. Acolytes are not normally asked to open the aumbry.

Sanctuary lamp: Close to the aumbry or tabernacle you may find a candle or oil lamp that burns at all times throughout the year. The light reminds us that Christ is present in the consecrated elements. The only time the sanctuary light is extinguished is after the Maundy Thursday service, when the altar is stripped for Good Friday. It is relit after the Easter Vigil.

In the Nave

Baptismal font and holy water font: The baptismal font is a stand with a basin for holding water during a Baptism. The font can be made of marble in one piece and can be quite elaborate or as simple as a table and ceramic basin. The holy water font can be a separate stand with basin, or a small half-basin attached to the wall near the entry to the nave. Historically, baptismal fonts were placed in the back of the nave and close to the door as a reminder that it is through Baptism that we enter the Christian community. When entering the church, we are encouraged to dip a finger in the holy water and make the sign of the cross on our own forehead as a reminder of the promises made at our Baptism and renewed at our Confirmation.

Stations of the cross: A series of plaques placed at intervals on the walls of the nave tell the story of Jesus' journey to the crucifixion and resurrection. These are used mostly during Lent for a short service in which participants walk from station to station to hear a piece of the story at each and share prayers.

Other Items

Never be afraid to ask your priest (or a member of the altar guild) to explain the purpose and uses of vestments and equipment that you aren't sure about or don't recognize. The more you know and understand, the better job you can do as an acolyte. More information is also available in the books and websites listed in the Suggested Reading section.

Chapter 3
Traditional Acolyte Duties: How and What We Do

Being an acolyte requires more than just wearing red vestments, lighting candles, and leading processions. Acolytes perform a variety of duties that support the worship service and free the priest to celebrate the Eucharist and guide worship. Yet they move through the service so quietly that the worshipers themselves hardly notice most of the duties they perform. Many of those duties are age-old and still performed in the traditional ways. However, most traditions have practical roots, as you will find in the descriptions below. Well before the service begins and after the last candle has been snuffed, acolytes are still busy.

General Expectations

Not surprisingly, the general expectations for acolytes are similar from parish to parish and are also purely practical. Some of these are listed here:

- When scheduled to serve, you should arrive fifteen to twenty minutes before a service. This allows you to vest without rushing and review any changes in the service before it begins.
- Always check your equipment as soon as you are vested. Knowing that the torch stands are in the right place or that the proper items are on the credence table prevents potential problems during the service.
- Always check with the senior acolyte or acolyte leader before each service to see if there are any changes or special requirements.
- Wear black or dark shoes and dark pants and socks or plain stockings under vestments. As acolytes, we do our best to move through the service with as little distraction to worshipers as

possible. White, high-top sneakers with a neon blaze or sandals that slap against your feet call attention to the wearer.

- Make sure your vestments are neat, clean, and hemmed approximately six inches off the floor so that you can go up and down steps without tripping. Hang up your vestments neatly after the service.
- If you can't serve when scheduled, you are still responsible for seeing that your place is filled. Try to find a replacement, and if you can't find someone willing to serve for you, call the acolyte leader for assistance.

The Servant Attitude

In order to move through the service quietly and without drawing attention to yourself, adapt the servant attitude.

- When not directly in use, your hands should be folded at or slightly above waist level.
- Never watch the faces of the worshipers, especially at Communion. People can feel it when they are being watched, and it is distracting.
- Learn to use silent language on the altar. For example, when the priest is finished with the breadbox, he or she bows slightly to the acolyte in an unspoken gesture that says, "I'm done, thank you." Your bow in return says, "You're welcome." If you forget something, the priest will often point and then open his or her hands in a palm-up gesture that says, "I need that now." Acolytes often use the same open-hand gesture to say, "I'll hold that for you."
- Know what is expected of you before the service. Ask questions if you're not sure. Be certain of the cues. For example, if you're asked to lead the families to the baptismal font at a certain hymn, ask if you should be in position and moving at the beginning of the first verse or wait until the last verse.
- Always move at a smooth, even pace. Rushing draws attention to yourself and increases the possibility of bumping into things or people, tripping, or dropping things.

Leading By Example

During the low Middle Ages when the language of church services was changed from Greek to Latin, acolytes were often chosen because they spoke that language and could answer the priest with the responses of the people during the Mass. Today services are held in the language of the local population, but worship leaders still rely on acolytes to begin the responses and to know when to kneel, stand, or sit during the service and how to behave respectfully in the sanctuary. Visitors particularly watch the acolytes to know what to do. To provide that leadership and be a good example for the congregation, you should do the following:

- When crossing in front of or behind the altar, always reverence the cross (either bow from the waist or genuflect). The exception to this rule is when you are carrying something, such as a torch or processional cross.
- In portions of the service when the priest(s) is seated, wait for him or her to sit first. This is a simple practice that shows respect for the clergy and your willingness to follow their example.
- Follow the priest's example of when to cross yourself or bow.
- When kneeling, keep your back straight and do not lean back against the chair or sit on your heels.
- Stand and sit up straight, and pay attention to the service. Don't slouch or daydream during the sermon.
- Treat your duties with reverence and respect and remember at all times that it is God whom you serve.

When all the members of the altar party project an attitude of reverence, the congregation will likewise respond, and the service is enriched for everyone.

Lighting and Tending the Altar Candles

Candles symbolize the light of Christ in the world. The two individual candles on the altar are the epistle and the gospel candle. When facing the altar from the nave or the congregational side of the altar, the epistle candle is on the right, and the gospel candle is on the left. Together these two candles are the eucharistic candles. The Paschal candle that represents the risen Christ, the Advent wreath, and individual hand candles for the congregation may also be used for specific services.

The altar candles are generally lit fifteen minutes before the formal beginning of the service. This is a time of meditation and preparation for worshipers. To light the candles, approach the altar, inside the rail, carrying the lighted lighter/snuffer, bow from the waist to reverence the altar, then step up to a point at which you can reach both candles. If the Paschal candle is present, light it first. If not, bring the lighter to the outside edge of the epistle side of the altar, light the epistle candle, and move the lighter back off the edge of the altar. Move the lighter around to the gospel side—and NOT across the altar cloth—repeat the process and light the gospel candle. (If you make the mistake of moving the lighter across the altar, you risk dripping wax on the altar cloth.) Then step back and again reverence the altar before returning to the sacristy to put away the lighter/snuffer. As a reminder of the proper order, just remember that "the gospel candle never stands alone." Light the gospel candle last and extinguish it first.

To extinguish the altar candles, approach the altar at a dignified pace, bow from the waist, step up, and then place the bell of the snuffer just over the follower (the brass cap on the top of the candle) on the gospel candle and count to three. This should be enough time for the flame to die. Pressing the bell down too far presses the wick into the wax and makes the candle difficult to light again without trimming. Again, bring the snuffer around to the epistle side of the altar and snuff that candle. Then step back and reverence the altar again before retreating to the sacristy. If possible, leave the Paschal candle burning until the congregation has left and then return to extinguish it.

Order for Lighting Altar Candles

* Move the lighter/snuffer over the short edge of the altar and not across it.
*When the Paschal candle is present, light it first.

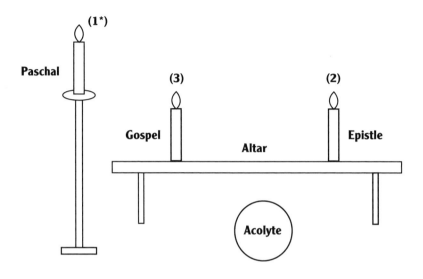

Order for Extinguishing Altar Candles

*When the Paschal candle is present, snuff it after the congregation has been dismissed.

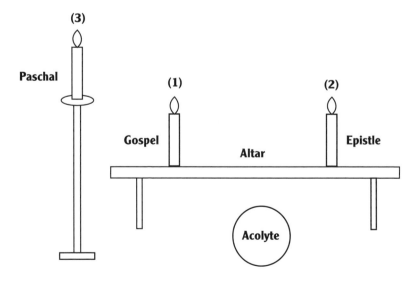

Many churches also use six additional service candles or office lights on the altar or on a candle rail behind and above the altar. They are usually arranged in a candelabrum or separate holders with three candles on each side of the altar. These are lit for Morning Prayer and for all altar-based liturgies. In a parish that uses office lights, the gospel and epistle candles are lit only for eucharistic services. The service candles are lit and extinguished after the eucharistic candles. To remember the order for lighting these, think of a set of curtains—beginning on the epistle side, start at the center of the altar and move to the outside as if you were drawing back a curtain. Then light the gospel side, again moving from the center to the outside. Conversely, at the end of the service, close the curtains by starting from the outside of the gospel side and moving toward the center; then repeat for the other side. The order of lighting is shown below.

Order for Lighting Altar Candles with Office Lights

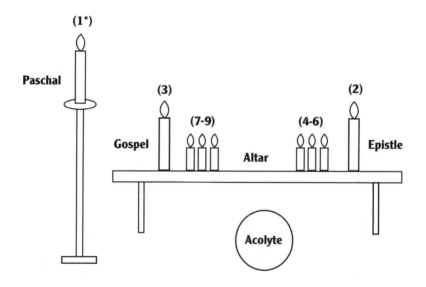

Order for Extinguishing Altar Candles with Office Lights

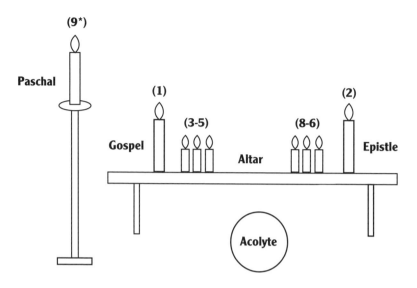

If hand candles or congregational candles are used, one to four acolytes light their own hand candles from either the Paschal candle or the eucharistic candles and proceed down the church aisles, lighting the hand candles of the first person in each pew and asking them to light the candle of the person sitting next to them. In this way, we share the light of Christ. To minimize wax drips on pew covers when lighting the candles of others, hold your candle upright while the other person tips their unlit candle to catch the flame.

Carrying Candles in Processions

Candles carried in procession are generally set in stands at prearranged positions close to the altar (those with staffs) or on the altar table itself (those in candle holders). If the candles are used to illuminate the cross or crucifix that leads the procession into the sanctuary, they should be carried with the flames even with each other and just under the cross piece on the processional cross.

Carrying the torch requires practiced balance. Lift the torch with two hands. Place one hand holding the staff at belt level and brace it against

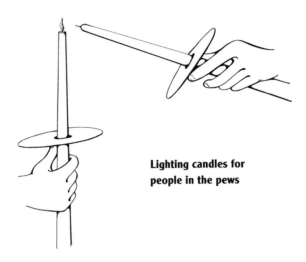

**Lighting candles for
people in the pews**

your waist. Your other hand should grip the staff at a point just under the bridge of your nose. Hold your elbow parallel to the floor (sticking straight out). Pull the torch in close to your body for maximum stability. This will keep the candle or taper upright and level while you walk or climb steps. Processional torches usually have drip plates, but can still drip hot wax on your vestments or in your hair if not kept steady.

Two torchbearers (the acolyte carrying the lighted candle can also be called simply a torch or taper) usually work as a team and mirror each other's movements. Learn to watch each other out of the corner of your eyes so that you can walk and climb stairs at the same pace and turn corners together. With practice, you will be able to mirror each other's movements from opposite sides of the altar or even from opposite sides of the church.

Leading Processions

A procession signals either a formal beginning or ending to our services but also helps to create an atmosphere of celebration and joy for worship.

Leading a procession is a big job. Before ever lifting the processional cross, you have to see that all participants are present and ready to process and if not, ask for help in finding the missing person or group. You also need to make sure that the standard step-off cue (the cue you use to step forward and begin the procession—often the second verse of the processional hymn) is appropriate for the length of the procession. A short hymn can leave people stranded in the aisle after the music has ended. You must also know the exact route being used for a particular service and set the pace so that everyone in the procession reaches his or her seat by the end of the hymn.

The basic method for carrying or balancing the processional cross is to lift it with two hands, like the torch, putting one hand at belt or waist level and the top hand just under the bridge of your nose (so that you can see over it). Pull the staff in against your body for stability. The wrist on your upper hand should be turned in and the elbow should be parallel to the

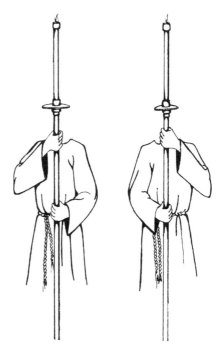

Holding a torch correctly

ground and perpendicular to the body. The old tradition of turning the wrist outward looks good, but may cause shoulder strain for young people.

On reaching the altar area with the procession, you place the cross in a special stand either in the sanctuary or sacristy and go directly to your seat.

A different set of cues is used for the retiring procession. For example, for a routine Sunday service, the cue might be the beginning of the final hymn. At that point you would go get the cross and, with the torchbearers, position yourself in front of the altar to wait for the first participants to join you before stepping off. See the crucifier chapter for a closer look at how cues and timing come together in a smooth procession.

The Gospel Procession

If your parish has a deacon, he or she will most likely process the gospel book. If not, you may be asked to do this.

At whatever cue has been established (for example, the last verse of the gospel hymn), pick up the gospel book from the altar and carry it to the center of the sanctuary (count the pews and establish a specific pew number to be used as the center) or a designated place in your particular church. Move at a stately pace. Carry the book on your forearms with your fingers curled over the bottom edge of the book. Make sure the book is face up with the cross on the front cover showing. If torchbearers are used, they will follow you to the center of the sanctuary and position themselves either beside or behind you, depending on the space available. When you reach the right spot, turn and face the altar.

When holding the book for the priest or deacon to read, brace your elbows against your rib cage with the book resting on your outstretched forearms. When the priest or deacon opens the book and rests it on your arms, curl your fingers upward and over the bottom edge of the book to hold the page. The priest or deacon will then read the gospel selection for the day, raise the book, close it, and lay it back on your forearms. He or she will then step aside to allow you and the torches to lead the procession back to the altar. Replace the book on the altar and return to your seat.

Special Processions with the Canterbury Square

One of the most beautiful ceremonial processions is the Canterbury Square with four torches. This configuration can be used to highlight the gospel reading, to escort a visiting dignitary in the procession, and for other occasions as well. Here's what the Canterbury Square for a gospel reading looks like when the procession reaches the center of the church:

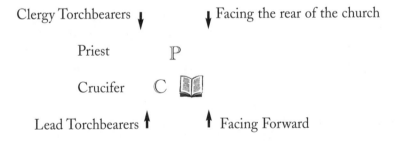

To start the gospel procession, all four torches go to their stands and wait. As soon as the clergy crucifer picks up the gospel book, the lead torchbearers (because their stands are in front) step-off, followed by the clergy torches. The lead torchbearers pass the crucifer and take up their positions behind him or her. The clergy torchbearers stop in front of the crucifer (leave at least two pews' width), and then turn to face each other and move back as far as possible against the pews to allow the priest to walk into the square. The clergy torchbearers then face forward to close the square. After the reading, the priest will step aside, and the crucifer alone walks between the clergy torchbearers to lead the square. The clergy torchbearers turn, face forward, and follow the crucifer. The lead torches follow behind.

To escort a dignitary, two torchbearers lead and two follow, keeping the dignitary centered in the moving square.

Handling the Alms Basin and/or Collection Plates

In most parishes the alms basin and/or collection plates are kept on or near the credence table. Bring the basins around and to the front of the altar to the ushers after the offertory sentence(s). In exchange, the ushers will generally give you the count of communicants present so that the priest or deacon can prepare enough bread and wine for the Eucharist. While the collection is going on, you help the priest or deacon prepare the table. After the table is prepared, return to the front of the altar, receive the alms basin, and carry it to the priest to be presented. The priest may return the basin to you right away or keep it on the altar throughout the Eucharist and return it to you to be put back on the credence table after the fraction or after Communion.

Preparing for the Eucharist

After taking the collection plates to the usher, help the deacon or priest prepare the table for the Eucharist. For larger services a second chalice may be needed. This may be delivered to the altar before the plates are given to the ushers or later after the fraction. If the ushers or other members of the congregation bring forward the gifts (bread and wine), take the collection plates to the rail, and with one hand, offer the plates and with the other hand, take the ciborium or breadbox. Place it on the credence table. Return to the ushers and take the water and wine to the credence table. In simpler services, the bread, wine, and water are already set out on the credence table.

A few general rules to rcmember while helping to prepare the table follow. First, lids and stoppers are left on the credence table. Second, most communication between the acolyte and clergy takes place in the unspoken language of the altar. For example, when the priest is finished with the breadbox, he bows slightly in a gesture that says, "I'm done, thank you." Your bow in return says, "I understand and you're welcome." If you forget something, the priest will often point and then open his or her hands in a palm-up gesture to say, "I need that now."

After everything is on the credence table, remove the lid from the breadbox, and take the box to the priest or deacon. Give him or her the number of communicants and hold out the box. Hold the box with two hands near the bottom. The priest or deacon will take what is needed from the box and then bow. Bow in return, and take the box back to the credence table and replace the lid.

Next carry both the water and wine cruets to the altar. Since the wine will be poured first, that cruet should be in your right hand with the handle facing the priest or deacon. Always give with the right hand and take back with the left hand. As soon as the priest takes the wine cruet, move the water to your right hand. Take the wine cruet back with your left hand, offer the water, and then move the wine to your right hand so that your left hand is free. The circular method of handling the cruets is age-old and may sound fussy but actually simplifies the process and limits the possibility of accidents while handling delicate articles. When both acolyte and priest know what to expect, their movements can be smooth and efficient. For some services, the priest may prefer to keep the wine cruet or a flagon (for larger services) on the altar and return only the water cruet to you.

After returning the cruet(s) to the credence table, pick up the lavabo bowl in your left hand, drape the small towel over your left wrist and forearm, pick up the water cruet by the handle with the right hand, and return to the altar to help the celebrant wash his or her hands. When you hold out the bowl, the priest will place his or her fingers over the bowl for you to pour water over them. Next, hold out your forearm to offer the towel. Keep the arm there until the celebrant replaces the towel. Return the lavabo bowl, towel, and cruet to the credence table, and replace the stoppers in the cruets. Go to the front of the altar to receive the alms basin or collection plates.

Fetching and Carrying

Listed above are the usual chores and duties acolytes perform; however, acolytes are servants of God and his Church. Your job may include almost anything needed to make the worship service flow more smoothly. For example, during a Baptism, you may be asked to hold the priest's prayer book, bring out the water at the appropriate moment, hand out baptismal certificates, light the baptismal candles from the Paschal candle, or remove extra tables or other items after the Baptism.

Festivals or Other Special Services

Festival or special services require a lot more work and knowledge on your part. The best way to prepare is to review the service in the Book of Common Prayer ahead of time and, if there is a rehearsal, be sure to attend. Some parishes assign two crucifers and two sets of torchbearers for a festival service so that one set leads the procession and another set leads the clergy. If four torchbearers are assigned, you may also work in a team to form the Canterbury Configuration or Square to light the gospel procession or light the path of a visiting dignitary. Some of the extra duties often include lighting hand candles, turning off overhead lights, and helping move furniture or equipment before or during the services. You may also be assigned as a thurifer, book bearer, boat bearer, or banner bearer. For details on those jobs, see Chapter 7.

Which Acolyte Does What

For simple services, one acolyte may be able to provide all the support necessary and perform the duties usually attributed to both the crucifer and the server. At other services, three, four, or more acolytes may be needed with the duties divided between them. Who does what specific job may be based on traditional divisions, such as the torchbearer, crucifer, and server, but may also depend on the number of acolytes available and their level of experience. Your ultimate goal is to enhance the worship service rather than to claim credit for a particular duty.

Everyone Makes Mistakes

It's important to understand that we all make mistakes. At an acolyte festival in 1997, a visiting bishop told about his own worst moment as an acolyte. On an Easter Sunday, he was carrying a very full alms basin to the priest to be presented when he tripped on the altar steps. Bills, checks, and envelopes fluttered to the floor while quarters, dimes, and nickels rolled down the aisles and under the pews. Half the congregation got on their hands and knees to help retrieve the money. It was every acolyte's worst nightmare, but the bishop kept his composure—and his sense of humor. When we'd all finished laughing, the bishop told us that if God did not smite him for that, there wasn't much we could do that would bring down the Almighty's wrath.

Mistakes and accidents happen to everyone. The important lesson is to respond to our own, and the mistakes of others, with grace (not hysteria), to learn from them, and to try not to make the same mistake twice.

Notes:

Chapter 4
The Torchbearer

Candlelight represents the light of Christ in the world. Your job is to carry that light and make it part of our worship.

This chapter details the actions of the torchbearer (also called the torch or taper) step-by-step through a Sunday morning worship service. All parishes are slightly different however, so space has been included for you to write in the details and cues particular to your own parish.

Before the Sunday Service

- Arrive early and vest at least fifteen to twenty minutes before the service is scheduled to begin. This may mean leaving home a little early or slipping out of Sunday school before class ends.
- Check your vestments for proper length. The bottom of your vestments should be a minimum of six inches from the floor so you can go up and down steps without tripping.
- Once you're vested, take your torch and go directly to the waiting area and find your partner and the crucifer.
- Your torch should be lighted five minutes before the procession. If the crucifer has not done this, do it yourself or ask one of the other service team members to help you.
- Keep your eye on the crucifer; he or she will tell you when to line up for procession.
- Before the procession begins, you and your partner should turn, face each other, and check that the drip plates on your torches are even and that the flames are just under the cross bar of the processional cross.

Notes:

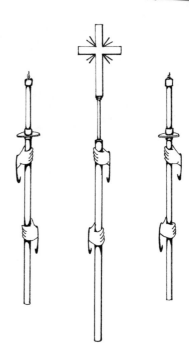

Processional cross and torches

During the Service

- The crucifer normally begins processions, so take your cues from him or her. Move shoulder to shoulder with the crucifer or, depending on the width of the aisle, with your partner directly behind the crucifer. Maintain an even steady pace with each other and the crucifer. When you reach the altar rail, go straight ahead or left and right as needed to put your torches into their stands for the service. Remember to mirror each other; you are a team!

Parish cue and route:

- Only hand and eye signals are generally used on the altar, so stay alert to catch changes in the service routine or requests for help from the server or crucifer.

Parish hand signals:

- For the gospel procession, go to your assigned torch stand as the gospel hymn begins. Wait for the crucifer to pick up the gospel book from the altar, and then step forward with your partner. Check your partner and step off opposite sides of the altar at the same time. Move at a steady pace to the front of the altar and turn together to process down the aisle. Pass the crucifer, turn and stand on either side of him or her, or together just behind him or her, with your torches resting on the floor. After the gospel has been read, follow the crucifer back to the altar, again moving as a team. Replace your torches in the stands and take your seats.

Parish cue and route:

- For Communion, line up with the other service team members. If you do not wish to receive, cross your hands over your chest, and the priest will bless you instead. Then quietly kneel at your seats. Do *not* watch the faces of the communicants at the rail.

Parish cue:

- As the recessional hymn begins, go immediately to your torch stands. As soon as the crucifer clears the sacristy doorway, step off together, and move to the center front of the altar. Line up on either side of the crucifer, facing toward the altar. Leave enough room for the crucifer to turn easily. Turn around together when the crucifer turns to face forward, and as soon as the crucifer steps off, move in shoulder to shoulder for the exit procession.

Parish cue:

• Wait quietly in the back of the church for the dismissal. Afterward, return your torch to its stand.

Parish cue:

After the Service

• Hang your vestments neatly. If they are dirty, have wax drips, or need repair, place them in the hamper or tell the acolyte leader.
• If you notice any problems with your torch or stand, please point it out to the acolyte leader after the service.

Notes:

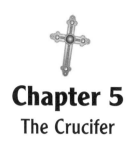

Chapter 5
The Crucifer

You tend the altar and carry the cross of Christ. You lead us into worship and lead us out into the world again. You also help set the tone for the worship service. How well you do your job can be measured by how well the congregation focuses on worship and not on you.

In this chapter, you can follow the actions of the crucifer step-by-step through a Sunday morning service. All parishes are slightly different, however, so space has been included for you to write in the details and cues particular to your parish.

Before the Service

- Be vested at least _____ minutes before the service.
- Light the altar candle fifteen minutes before the service is scheduled to begin. If necessary, review the order for lighting in Chapter 3. The rule of thumb for candles is, "If it's there, light it." The only exception are those in the Advent wreath.

Notes:

- Check to see that the torchbearers have arrived _____ minutes before the service begins; discuss with the server, acolyte leader, or priest whether you should find a replacement or go without torch bearers for the service. One torchbearer usually does not serve alone because it makes the procession appear unbalanced and draws attention away from the cross.

Notes:

- Check with the server to see if there are changes to the routine, and if there are, inform the torches. If there is a deacon present, he or she will read the gospel. If there are two or more priests (and no deacon), ask which one will read the gospel.
- Check the equipment you expect to use for the service. Help the torches check and refill oil torches or change tapers (candles) if needed. Oil for the liquid torches, fresh candles, and wicks for the lighter/snuffer, and so forth are located _____.
- Double-check your step-off cue for the procession. Often, the cue will be the second verse of a processional hymn. If it is a short hymn, you may need to discuss with the priest changing the step-off cue to the first verse. For a silent procession, such as those used in Lent or for funerals, the cue will often be a slow count to ten after the prelude ends. Check the bulletin to know what prelude music to expect.

Notes:

- Five minutes before the procession, light the torches. At this point your priest may gather everyone for prayer. Afterward, signal the torchbearers to line up for the procession. Position yourself and the

torchbearers a few feet from the door to the sanctuary so
that latecomers can still enter. When the choir or others in the
procession see you do this they will almost automatically begin
lining up. Check to see that all members of the procession are there
and in the right order. If the junior choir is present, make sure the
choir director knows what cues you intend to use, especially for the
retiring procession.

Notes:

- Just before you step off, raise the cross and turn to face the
torchbearers so that all of you can check the height of the torches
and adjust them if necessary. Listen carefully for your cue so that
you step off at the right moment.

Notes:

During the Service

- Carry the cross high! See Chapter 3 for information on carrying and
balancing the processional cross. Lead the procession slowly and
with dignity. Remember that the choir and clergy behind you will
tend to walk in time to the slowest cadence of the music and must
read a hymnal while they walk. Don't run away from them! If you
notice the singing becoming fainter, slow down! Although they are

supposed to follow your lead and pace, a smooth procession is a joint
effort by all concerned.

- Process straight to the altar rail before turning right to put the cross
in the stand. Then go to your position on the altar and reverence
with the rest of the service team.

Parish cue and route:

- During the service, occasionally check the torchbearers and server
visually. If the torchbearers have forgotten a cue, just a glance will
generally remind them. If the server needs assistance, he or she will
signal you. Provide whatever assistance the server or priest needs.
Participate in the service, but stay alert!

Notes:

- At a prearranged cue, such as the last verse of the gospel hymn,
begin the gospel procession. Check the torchbearers to make sure
they are ready and paying attention. Step forward and pick up the
gospel book from the altar and lead the torchbearers and priest or
deacon to the center of the church (count the pews to give yourself
a stopping point). The torchbearers will line up behind you or beside
you if there is space in the aisle. You now become a bookstand! Some
clergy will want you to hold the book while they read from it.
Others will hold it themselves. At the end of the reading, the
priest will step to one side to allow you and the torchbearers to pass.
Holding the book face up on your forearms, return it to the altar.

Gospel cue:

- At Communion, line up with the other service team members to receive Communion. If you do not wish to receive, cross your hands over your chest as a signal to the priest and chalice bearer, and the priest will bless you instead. Return to your seat and kneel at your place. Do *not* watch the faces of communicants at the rail.

Notes:

- At a prearranged cue, often the beginning of the last or recessional hymn, get the cross and stand in front of and facing the altar. The torchbearers will line up beside you. When the first choir members have completely turned the corner of the altar rail, turn slowly, and lead the procession out of the sanctuary. Walk slowly and give the torchbearers and choir time to line up properly behind you.

Notes:

- At the end of the procession, put your cross in the stand or hand it off to one of the torchbearers, and go immediately up the side aisle. Get the snuffer and extinguish the candles on the altar. The priest or deacon will often wait for you to do this before pronouncing the dismissal. Don't rush, even if the music has ended. Walk at a dignified but deliberate pace.

Notes:

After the Service

- Hang your vestments neatly. If they are dirty, have wax drips, or need repair, put them in the hamper or tell the acolyte leader.
- If you had any problems during the service or noticed equipment that needs repair, make sure you tell the acolyte leader after the service.

Notes:

Chapter 6
The Server

As the server, you are the personal servant to the priest and work closely with the sacraments at the heart of the service. The more experienced and comfortable you become, the more invisible your part in the service will be.

You may also be the senior acolyte for the service. This implies both responsibility and authority. The other acolytes will look to you for guidance. Make sure you share any changes in the service routine, and make eye contact with them occasionally during the service.

In this chapter, follow the actions of the server step-by-step through a Sunday-morning service. All parishes are slightly different, however, so space has been included for you to write in the details and cues particular to your parish.

Before the Service

- Arrive at least _____ minutes before the service so that you have time to vest without rushing.
- Always ask the priest for any changes or additional instructions and make sure team members (if any) understand the changes.
- You also need to know who will prepare the altar (if a deacon and priest or two priests are present) and which priest will celebrate. The celebrant is usually the one wearing the chasuble (the large oval vestment); other clergy assisting in the service will be wearing a stole.
- Check the credence table and make sure all the equipment you will need has been set out.

- The altar candles should be lighted fifteen minutes before the service. If a crucifer has been assigned, check to see that this is done. If you are serving alone, light the candles yourself.
- Check to see that the crucifer and torches have arrived and are vested. If a scheduled acolyte is missing, decide whether to replace that person or go without. You can double as a crucifer, thurifer, or torch.

Notes:

During the Service

- The procession for a simple or "low mass" service is usually informal and begins and ends in the sacristy. When you exit the sacristy, the order is first acolyte, then chalice bearer or lay minister, and then the priest. If you pass a small altar, stop and reverence as a group. Then proceed to the main altar, stopping just past the center and directly behind it. The chalice bearer stops on the far side of the altar, and the priest moves to the center. Reverence the altar together. Then step back and go to your seat. For a more formal service, the procession begins in the back of the church and is lead by a crucifer and torch bearer. Process in the rear of the procession in front of the priest(s). If you are doubling as the crucifer or as a torchbearer, see Chapters 4 and 5.

Parish cue and route:

- Participate in the service. Members of the congregation who aren't sure whether to kneel, sit, or stand will watch you and the other service team members and follow your example.
- After the priest gives the offertory sentences, go to the credence table and begin preparing for the Eucharist. First, take the collection plates to the usher. He or she will give you the number of possible communicants present for the service.

Notes:

- For a small or simple service, the bread, wine, and water will be laid out on the credence table. For larger or more formal services, the ushers may bring forward the bread, wine, and water. In this case, hand the alms basin or collection plates to the usher with one hand and take the breadbox or ciborium. Take the bread to the credence table. Return to the ushers and take the wine and water cruets and put them on the credence table. Then continue as follows.
- Remove the lid from the breadbox or ciborium and take it to the priest or deacon who is preparing the altar. Hold it with both hands at the bottom of the box or by the stem and bottom. Give the priest or deacon the number of communicants. Wait until the priest bows to signal that he or she has finished with the bread box before you bow in return and take the box back to the credence table.
- Next, take the wine and water to the altar (both handles toward the priest). Always give with the right hand, take with the left. Wait for him or her to return the cruets to you. The priest will then bow. Bow in return, and replace the cruets on the credence table. For a large service, a flagon of wine may be used either instead of or as well as a cruet. The priest may keep the flagon or the wine cruet on the altar and return only the water cruet to you. Return the cruet(s) to the credence table.
- Take the lavabo towel from the credence table and drape it over

your left forearm (like a waiter), pick up the lavabo bowl from the table with your left hand and the water cruet (by the handle) with your right hand. Go to the primary celebrant (not necessarily the same person who prepared the altar). He or she will hold his or her fingers over the lavabo bowl so that you can pour water over them (over the bowl). Next, hold your left forearm out for him or her to take the towel. Keep your forearm held out until he or she replaces the towel. Replace the equipment on the credence table.

- Collect the alms basins or collection plates from the ushers, walk around the altar, and give them to the priest to be offered. Then put the alms basins back on the lower shelf of the credence table.

Notes:

- If your parish uses Sanctus bells, ring them three times, once at each "Holy" in the Sanctus acclamation. If the acclamation is sung, the bells are not normally used. The bells also mark solemn moments in the Eucharist as the priest tells the story of the last supper. Ring the bells as the priest holds up the Host each time after he or she says the words "Do this for the remembrance of me."

Notes:

- If a second chalice is needed, bring this quietly to the priest after the fraction (breaking of the bread).

Notes:

- Cleaning up (called ablutions). After the last person has received Communion wine, take the water (you have the handle), and wait behind the altar out of the way. The priest will generally nod at you when he or she is ready to have you bring the water. Step forward and pour the water into the chalice. Wait until the priest bows (you may need to pour twice or for a second chalice) before returning the cruet to the credence table. If the second chalice, a flagon, or other extra equipment is still on the altar, go and stand at the edge of the altar and wait to be handed items that need to be returned to the credence table. If the vessels are to be cleaned after the service, the priest will cover the chalice(s) and paten with a pall; then the priest, the deacon, or you will put them on the credence table or in the sacristy.

Notes:

- An informal exit procession begins after the blessing. Join the priest and chalice bearer or deacon to reverence the altar, then turn and lead the others off the altar. Return to the sacristy, remove your cotta, and immediately return to the altar to extinguish the candles. A formal exit for a larger service usually includes a procession with the crucifer, torchbearers, choir, chalice bearers or lay ministers, and priest as well as other possible service participants, to the back of the church. Process in front of the priest(s).

Notes:

- After a formal procession (unless you are also the crucifer), stay close to the priest(s) so you can take the chasuble, stole(s), and prayer book(s) immediately after the dismissal and return them to the sacristy so that the priest(s) can comfortably greet parishioners leaving church.

Notes:

After the Service

- After you hang up or put away the priest's vestments, hang up your own vestments neatly. If your vestments are dirty or stained with wax, put them in the hamper or tell the acolyte leader.
- Ask the other acolytes if they have any questions, and if so, answer them or refer them to the acolyte leader. Also ask if they noticed any problems with equipment or service cues. If the acolytes did a particularly good job, tell them so and pass that information along to the acolyte leader.

Notes:

Chapter 7
Other Acolyte Jobs

Depending on the parish and the particular type of service, you may be asked to serve in a specialized position. Some parishes use one or more of these positions routinely, others use them only for special or festival services. If you are assigned to a special position, discuss the specific duties with your acolyte leader and take notes on a card to review later or tuck them into your prayer book for the service. If there is a rehearsal scheduled, you should attend if it is at all possible.

The Thurifer

The thurifer carries the incense in procession and to prepare for the Eucharist. During the rehearsal, practice the three-swing rhythm with the thurible, the full 360-degree swing, or figure-eight revolutions (the priest will decide which is appropriate) until you are comfortable with the motions and can control the thurible. Also ask if the priest will want you to cense him or her and the congregation during the service.

Before the Service

- Put charcoal in the thurible and light it at least twenty minutes before the service. Charcoal can be difficult to light and its heat spreads slowly. To make cleaning up easier, line the cup inside the thurible with aluminum foil before adding the charcoal.
- Check with the crucifer for the opening cue for the procession. Five minutes before the start of the procession, present the thurible to the priest to add incense. The priest will normally bless and add incense

for both the entry procession and censing the altar, but may also ask you to add extra incense before the exit procession.

Notes:

- Make sure either the boat bearer or server has the boat and will carry it in the procession and put it on the credence table.
- Make sure you know where the thurible is to be kept during the service so that it's not a fire hazard. The spot needs to be fireproof.

Notes:

During the Service

- Lead the procession slowly and with dignity, using the censing method decided before the service.
- When you're not using the thurible during the service, store it in the sacristy sink or other fireproof spot that has been decided upon earlier. Do not try to keep it with you for the entire service.

Notes:

- Preparing the altar: During the announcements, go to the sacristy and add another charcoal to the thurible. As soon as the priest announces the offertory sentences, go stand beside the credence table out of the server's path and wait. Hold the boat in one hand (leave the lid on the credence table) and the thurible in the other. If a boat bearer has been assigned, he or she will hold and offer the boat. The priest will nod when he or she is ready for you to step up to the altar. Offer the boat and he or she will add incense before taking the thurible to cense the altar. Put the lid back on the boat and place it on the credence table. Depending on what was decided beforehand, the priest may ask either the deacon or you to cense him or her. If you are to cense the priest, swing the thurible gently three times toward the priest. If you are to cense the congregation, go to the front of the altar rail and again swing the thurible three times. When you are finished, turn and reverence the altar before you return to the sacristy and put the thurible back in the sink or whatever fireproof spot was chosen before the service.

Notes:

- To prepare for the exit procession, retrieve the thurible as the final hymn begins. Add another charcoal and one-half spoonful of incense to the thurible. The priest may have you bring the boat to him or her to add the incense (check about this before the service).
- For the exit procession, position yourself in front of the altar, between the crucifer and the congregation. As soon as the crucifer turns to face you, turn and immediately begin the procession. He or she will allow you at least six paces before following.

After the Service

- Clean the thurible. Empty the charcoal outside onto bare ground, a stone step, or gravel (but not on a walkway). Make sure the charcoal is completely cold before you leave it. Once the thurible has cooled, wipe out the cup that holds the charcoal with a damp cloth.

Notes:

The Boat Bearer

The boat bearer or boat carries the incense in processions and for the preparation for the Eucharist.

Before the Service

- If there is a rehearsal, make sure you attend.
- Arrive at least twenty minutes early for the service. Vest and ask about any last-minute changes in the service.
- Make sure the boat is at least three-quarters full of incense before carrying it to the procession assembly area. Check that the thurifer has the charcoal started and ask if he or she needs any assistance. The incense is stored _____.

During the Service

- Process behind the thurifer. Allow the thurifer at least six to eight paces before you follow and keep that distance for both the entry and exit processions.
- Carry the boat in two hands. It is an offering. Place the boat on the credence table as soon as you reach the altar.
- During the announcements, when the thurifer goes to stand beside

the credence table, get the boat and stand beside him or her. When the priest nods, you will both step up to the altar. As soon as the thurifer opens the thurible, remove the lid from the boat and hold out the boat with the spoon facing the priest. Wait beside the thurifer until the priest bows to dismiss you. After the altar has been censed, and when the thurifer goes to put the thurible away, place the boat on the credence table and return to your seat.

Notes:

- As soon as the final hymn begins, take the boat to the sacristy so that the thurifer can add incense. Alternatively, you and the thurifer may again present the thurible to the priest to be filled. If so, offer the boat as before. Then follow the thurifer to the front of the altar for the exit procession.

Notes:

After the Service

- Return the boat to the sacristy and hang your vestments neatly.

Notes:

The Banner Bearer

• The banner bearer represents the congregation.

Before the Service

• Arrive early and check in with the crucifer or acolyte leader. Whether you wear vestments or street clothes will depend on the service. This decision will normally be made during rehearsal.
• Most banners are not particularly heavy, but their weight is balanced at the top. Lift the banner with two hands. Hook the thumb of the hand holding the bottom of the pole onto the front of your belt or brace it against your waistband. Slide the other hand up the pole to just under the bridge of your nose. Both hands should face inward. The bottom of the banner should be just over your head, and you should still be able to see clearly.
• Practice walking and balancing the banner. Also practice lowering the banner and tipping it to get though the sanctuary door, and then raising it again to processional height.
• Check the position of the banner stand in the front of the church immediately before the service.
• Check your assigned seating during the service.
• In processions the banner normally leads members of the congregation or the choir. Palm Sunday and Confirmation are examples. Check with the crucifer for your position in the procession before lining up.

Notes:

During the Service

- If the banner has a loop holding it to the bottom of the pole, unsnap it once you are through the sanctuary door to allow the banner to swing free.
- As the procession begins, allow the torches (or whoever is directly in front of you) to pass at least three pews before you step off (the distances will be decided before the service). Keep that distance for both the entry and exit procession. At the altar, turn left, place the banner in the stand (facing out), and go directly to your seat.

Notes:

- Be mindful of the pace of the procession. The rest of the procession will be moving at a stately (slower than normal) pace.
- The banner remains in the stand during the service.
- As soon as the final hymn begins, get the banner and stand near the end of the first pew to be ready for the exit procession. As soon as the torchbearers pass, move into the aisle and raise the banner. Allow them to pass at least three pews before you step off.

Notes:

After the Service

- Return the banner to the stand at the back of the church and snap the bottom loop.

Notes:

The Book Bearer

The book bearer or book carries the gospel book in procession and reminds us of the importance of the gospels in our lives.

Before the Service

- Attend the rehearsal if at all possible. Check the cues for the gospel procession and confirm whether two or four torchbearers will be included in the procession.
- If you are leading the gospel procession with the Canterbury Square or another special configuration, practice it before the service so that you know the cues, route, and pace. See Chapter 3 for a review of the Canterbury Square.
- Check your position in the procession. Generally you will be

directly in front of the lectors. Check also to see if the book will be included in the exit procession. It may not be.

- Get the book from the altar at least fifteen minutes before the service is scheduled to begin.

Notes:

During the Service

- Line up for the procession. Hold the bottom edge of the gospel book with both hands. The book should be upright with the cross on the front of the book showing.
- As soon as you reach the altar, place the book in its usual position on the altar and move to your seat.
- At a prearranged cue, often the last verse of the gospel hymn, go to the altar, pick up the book, and begin the gospel procession. If the gospel procession includes the Canterbury Square or another configuration, remember to move at a slightly slower pace.

Notes:

- At a prearranged cue, usually the third verse of the final hymn, pick up the gospel book and wait beside the priest or lectors until you can join in the procession at the right place.

Notes:

After the Service

- If the gospel book was included in the exit procession, return it to the altar or wherever it is stored when not in use. Hang up vestments neatly. If you noticed any problems with your cues or any of the altar equipment (not just the book), tell the acolyte leader.

Notes:

The Bishop's Server or Attendant

Many bishops travel with their own chaplain to act as server, while others do not. In that case, the parish may provide an associate priest, deacon, or a senior acolyte server to assist him or her.

Before the Service

- Meet the bishop at the door with your parish priest to be introduced and to offer your services. Offer to take the bishop's vestments and hang them up in the sacristy.
- The parish priest may offer a tour of your church or show the bishop to the sacristy or offer to have you do so while he or she gathers Confirmation families or other parishioners. If your parish priest is not available, act as host, offer refreshments, and introduce the bishop to parishioners.
- Offer the bishop a copy of the service bulletin and answer any questions about the service that you can.
- Before the procession, ask what the bishop would like you to do. He or she may ask you to carry the bishop's staff or crook in the procession and to take his or her cope and miter and hang them in the sacristy when they aren't needed. During the Confirmation portion of the service, he or she may need you to hold his or her prayer book or the small container of oil during the laying on of hands. Know beforehand what will be needed.

Notes:

During the Service

- Process directly in front of the bishop. If you carry the staff or crook for the procession, carry it in two hands, upright, and facing forward. When you arrive at the altar, lay it on the front edge of the altar and go to your seat.
- At a prearranged cue—for example, after the opening prayers and before the lessons—help the bishop remove his or her cope and miter and hang them in the sacristy. You will need to bring them back later in the service.
- During the service, you will probably be seated close by so you can offer extra assistance as needed.
- When the altar is prepared for the Eucharist, the regular server will assist the deacon or priest. But since the bishop will most likely be the celebrant, you will assist him or her with the lavabo.
- Before the final Communion prayer, retrieve the bishop's cope and miter from the sacristy and be ready to help him or her with them. The cope is heavy and can be difficult to put on in a hurry without help. Immediately retrieve the staff from the altar and give it to the bishop so that he or she has it for the final blessing.

Notes:

After the Service

- After the procession and dismissal, offer to take the bishop's vestments to the sacristy and hang them up so that he or she can greet parishioners.
- Hang your own vestments neatly and then return and stay unobtrusively near the bishop, offering any assistance needed, until his or her departure.

Notes:

Trainer or Mentor

A trainer or mentor is an experienced acolyte trusted to train new acolytes or those moving into new positions. If you are asked to be a trainer, ask your acolyte leader at least a day before the training session for a checklist or make notes of specific details that he or she wants you to cover. Arrive early for the training session and offer to help assemble equipment or help new acolytes to fit vestments. If you are a mentor, you may work specifically with one or two acolytes. You may then be asked help each acolyte vest for their first scheduled service, answer any last-minute questions, offer morale support, or even serve with him or her for that first service.

Notes:

Acolyte Roster

Write the names and phone numbers of fellow acolytes with whom you can trade services. If you cannot serve when you're scheduled and can't find a replacement, call the acolyte leader as soon as possible!

T = Torch   B = Banner bearer
C = Crucifer   Th = Thurifer
S = Server

	Name	Phone #/email
T/C/S	Carry A. Candle	unlisted carryc@noname.com
1.		
2.		
3.		
4.		
5.		
6.		
7.		
8.		

9.

10.

11.

12.

13.

14.

15.

16.

17.

18.

19.

20.

21.

22.

23.

24

25.

Suggested Reading

Learning as much as you can about your chosen ministry benefits both you and the church you serve. The following websites, books, and articles offer more in-depth information and fascinating (fun, too) reading on the subject of acolytes.

Valuable resources are available on the web but if you search on the word "acolyte," you may have to wade through several thousand references. However, there are a few particularly good sites. The Cathedral of the King website includes easily accessible and readable answers for almost any question about vestments and equipment used in the church (iccecsea.org/liturgy). The Lambeth Palace Library web site offers historical information about vestments (Lambethpalacelibrary.org). And for fast, down-to-earth answers on Episcopalian terminology check the Reverend John Burwell's glossary at http://www.holycross.net/anonline.htm.

Helpful books include the following:

Grun, Bernard. *The Timetables of History: The New Third Revised Edition.* New York: Simon and Schuster, 1991.

The Episcopal Church. The Book of Common Prayer. New York: The Church Hymnal Corporation, 1979. *Note:* Flip through this familiar book and read the rubrics (these are instructions in italics)and additional instructions provided for special services.

Heller, Christopher. *The New Complete Server.* Harrisburg, Pa.: Morehouse Publishing, 1995.

Michno, Dennis. *A Manual for Acolytes: The Duties of the Server at Liturgical Celebrations.* Wilton, Conn.: Morehouse-Barlow, 1981.

Price, Charles P. and Weil, Louis. *Liturgy for Living.* Harrisburg, Pa.: Morehouse Publishing, 2000.

Easily available articles on acolyte history include the following:

"Acolyte." *The Catholic Encyclopedia,* 1999 online edition.

"Acolyte." *Encyclopedia of the Lutheran Church,* vol. 1, 1999 ed.

"Altar Boy." *The New Catholic Encyclopedia.* Detroit: Thomson/Gale in association with the Catholic University, Washington, D.C., 1967.

"The History of the Office Of Acolytes." Adapted from "The History of Acolytes," by Pastor Belvin Brummett. The Trinity Lutheran Church website: www.tlc3n1.org/acolyte.html. 2002.